CONTENTS

JAN/FEB/MAR 2023

Celebrity Essential Oils by Alicia Robinson Cooper

Get Free in 2023! With Madeline Alexander, The Power Coach

....

Chad Lawson Cooper

FEATURED ARTICLE:
Chad Lawson Cooper
Justice on Trial

Excited doesn't even come close to sharing this moment I have been waiting for so long, To relaunch and introduce new and exciting articles and products tthat will be life changing for you the reader

We're More Than Conquerors Magazine is a God inspired idea that was   birthed in 2002 in a vision.

- Lady Katrina Haskins

Email k.haskins0128@gmail.com
Contact: 346-599-1240

Vincent Apartments

ALL BILLS PAID SERVICES PROVIDING FOR THE TENANTS TO DR.OFFICE VISITS,GROCERY STORE,SHOPPING STORE AREAS,WE ALSO PROVIDE IN THE ROOMS ARE SINGLE(DONT SHARE THE ROOMS)CABLE READY.

PLEASE CALL
THERESA WILLIAMS CHARLES
832-343-9842

WE ACCEPT DISABILITY BENEFITS ALSO AND DISABILITY CLIENTS.

Celebrity's Essentials
Handmade by Alicia Robinson Cooper
"FOR SKIN THAT'S SURE TO BE CELEBRATED"
Alicia Robinson Cooper
Celebritysessentials.com
•Organic products
•No presevatives
•24 hour moisture
•Rich in Omega 3's
•Good for eczema, dry and itchy skin
Vitamin E
Body
MANGO

You Can Begin Again

Written by Lady Katrina Haskins

The Bible is full of stories about new beginnings and verses about starting new. God knows that living under the curse of a fallen world is not easy for us. He understands that we fall down and long to begin again. He provides us encouragement and hope through His word.

If **you** don't like your answer, then let me give **you** some good news: It is never too late **to begin again!** Don't spend one more day living a narrow life that has room for only **you** and your fears. Make a decision right now that **you will** learn **to** live boldly, aggressively, and confidently. Don't let fear rule **you** any longer.

You Can Begin Again

Written by Lady Katrina Haskins

It's a terrible thing, I think, in life to wait until you're ready. I have this feeling now that actually no one is ever ready to do anything. There is almost no such thing as ready. There is only now." You could start again everyday, if you failed in your first second or even third attempt. There are no limitations on making new decisions and forming new goals. and there are no limitations on when to begin, go ahead and step out big or small just do it!

You can begin again by allowing God to shape your life by His skilled, purposeful, and loving hands. JEREMIAH 18:1-6

BEGINNING AGAIN

It's always easy to start again when you know that there is nothing you can't do. Every day is a new chance to start over and make it better. We're always going to have to start over, but the important thing is that we do. You can always start again. The only person who can stop you from starting is you.

As you're going through your journey of transition and beginning again, be sure you celebrate every step along the way. Acknowledge your courage and boldness at recreating your life and walking down a new path. It takes faith and trust to step out into the unknown. Be proud of yourself!

Organize your life. You can't change your life if you're living a crazy unorganized way. Once you know exactly what change you want to effect and what goals you want to reach, you can begin to plan to make the necessary changes. Take a new route. And remember with God all things are possible Philippians 4:13

Studying the stories of new beginnings in the Bible is one of the best ways to get ideas on how to move forward with God. Let's jump in… The first lesson about new beginnings in the Bible comes from the life of David. David is popular in the Scriptures for being a man after God's heart. Adultery (2 Samuel 11:4) although David did this and had a man killed, God still called David a man after my own heart so, no matter the situation we can begin again with GODS HELP!

Lady Katrina Haskins, Author

Chad Lawson Cooper

Meet Our Founder

Chad Everette Lawson Cooper (born February 17, 1971) is an American performer, filmmaker producer, director, writer, and composer who specializes in the gospel genre. In collaboration with Alicia Robinson Cooper, his wife of over 24 years. Reverend Cooper is the creator & writer of the nationally touring stage play: CHURCH MESS, which is billed as haven been the longest-running gospel stage play in the U.S.

Cooper is well known to theater audiences for his performances as William Gray in CHURCH MESS, and being the lead vocalist in the celebrated singing group Soul Tempo who was featured in the blockbuster film: THE PREACHERS WIFE. As a filmmaker, Cooper has produced & co-produced several feature films along with his wife Alicia Robinson Cooper, Hollywood Great Harry Lennix & Super Producer Mann Robinson. His stage plays are estimated to have grossed around $20 million in revenue YTD.

Dr. Cooper has worked with a pantheon of iconic gospel stars.and has been featured in several national publications, Cooper attended Florida A&M University and graduated from Springfield College. He earned his bachelor's degree in Philosophy and Religion and a Doctorate in Theology.

The Chad Cooper Company on Broadway is a professional theater and film company with a corporate office located at 42 Broadway, in the middle of Manhattan.

We have had great success with our 2 stage plays, which have been performed across the country, in over 100 series. Now, we have ventured into filmmaking. On February 16, 2020, The Chad Cooper Company, in conjunction with Justice on Trial The Movie 20/20 LLC., is set to release our feature film called "Justice" On Trial: The Movie 20/20, in AMC Theaters, as well as other venues across the country.

You can watch the trailer and learn more about the film on the official *justiceontrialthemovie.com*

DORIEN WILSON
TODD BRIDGES
DAVID ARQUILLA
JOHN GESMONDE
JUSTICE ON TRIAL
THE MOVIE
DIRECTED BY MANN ROBINSON

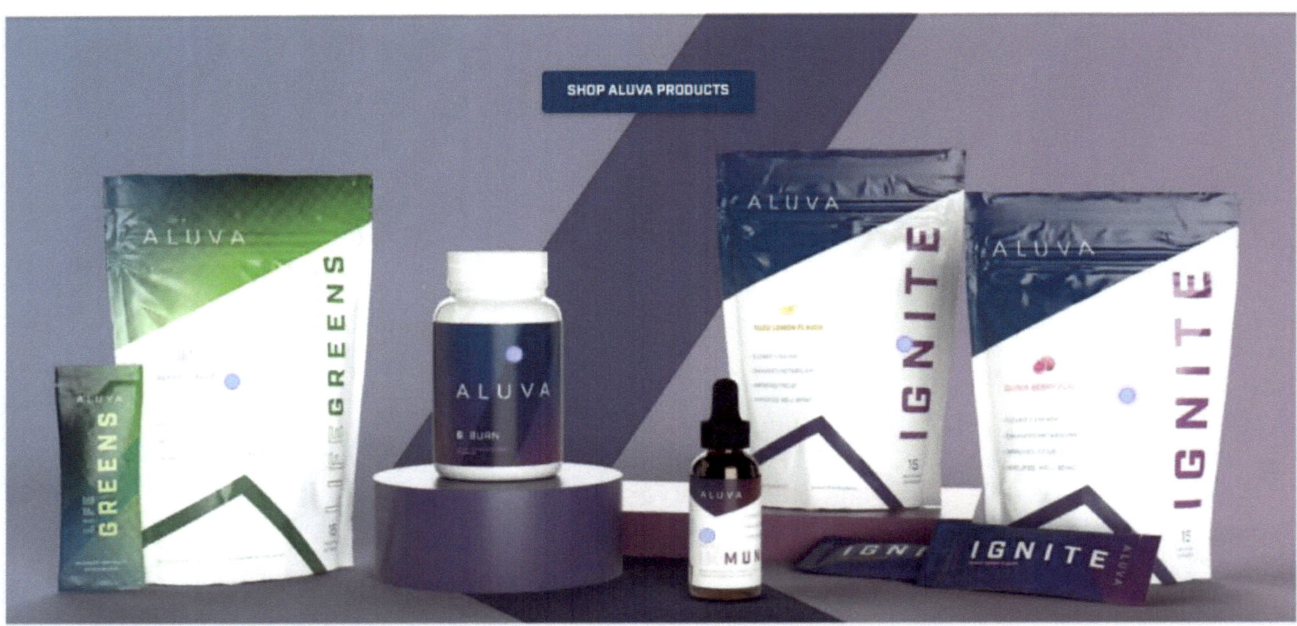

Your Website Link

https://aluva.co/e/cynthiadyer1950

Autumn
memories
Before
After
GLUCOSE IN RANGE
5:23 AM
155 mg/dL
GLUCOSE IN RANGE
88 mg/dL
Before
7:29 AM
176 mg/dL
After
107 mg/dL
PIC·COLLAGE
PIC·COLLAGE

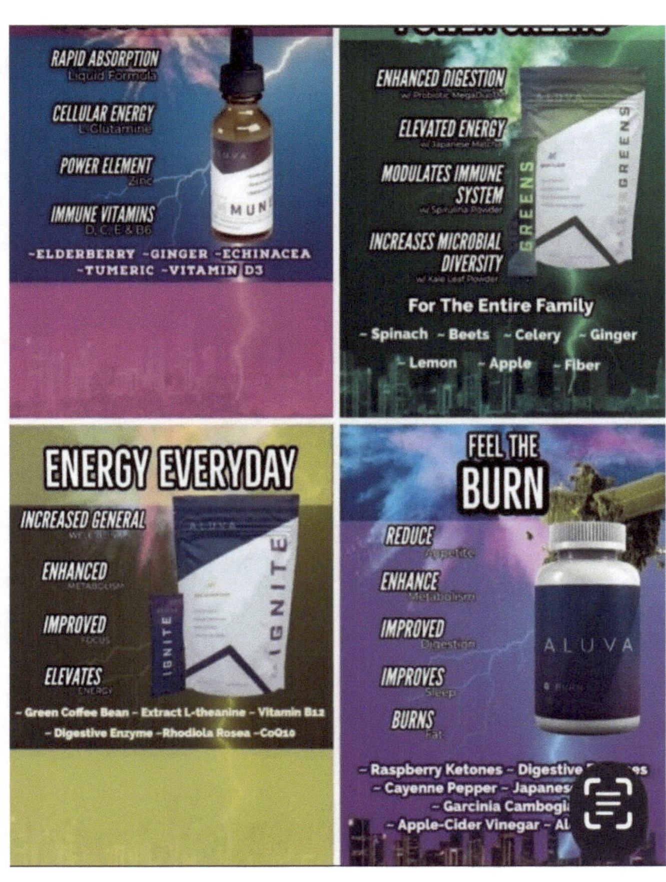
RAPID ABSORPTION
Liquid Formula
CELLULAR ENERGY
L-Glutamine
POWER ELEMENT
Zinc
IMMUNE VITAMINS
D, C, E & B6
~ELDERBERRY ~GINGER ~ECHINACEA
~TUMERIC ~VITAMIN D3
MUNE
ENHANCED DIGESTION
w/ Probiotic MegaDuo
ELEVATED ENERGY
w/ Japanese Matcha
MODULATES IMMUNE
SYSTEM
w/ Spirulina Powder
INCREASES MICROBIAL
DIVERSITY
w/ Kale Leaf Powder
GREENS
For The Entire Family
~ Spinach ~ Beets ~ Celery ~ Ginger
~ Lemon ~ Apple ~ Fiber
ENERGY EVERYDAY
INCREASED GENERAL
ENHANCED
METABOLISM
IMPROVED
FOCUS
ELEVATES
ENERGY
~ Green Coffee Bean ~ Extract L-theanine ~ Vitamin B12
~ Digestive Enzyme ~Rhodiola Rosea ~CoQ10
IGNITE
FEEL THE
BURN
REDUCE
Appetite
ENHANCE
Metabolism
IMPROVED
Digestion
IMPROVES
Sleep
BURNS
Fat
~ Raspberry Ketones ~ Digestive Enzymes
~ Cayenne Pepper ~ Japanese
~ Garcinia Cambogia
~ Apple-Cider Vinegar ~ Al
ALUVA

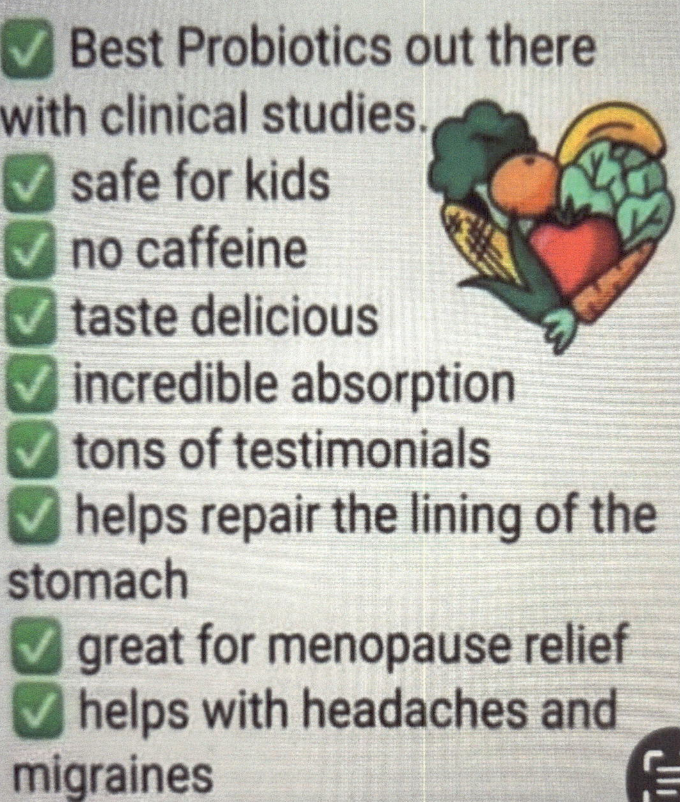
✅ Best Probiotics out there
with clinical studies.
✅ safe for kids
✅ no caffeine
✅ taste delicious
✅ incredible absorption
✅ tons of testimonials
✅ helps repair the lining of the
stomach
✅ great for menopause relief
✅ helps with headaches and
migraines

MOTTO

NO FIRST LADY LEFT BEHIND!

VISION STATEMENT

TO EDUCATE, ENCOURAGE, AND EMPOWER
WOMEN WORLDWIDE.

MISSION STATEMENT

TO BRING TOGETHER WOMEN FROM AROUND THE WORLD TO
CONNECT, ENCOURAGE, EDUCATE, EMPOWER, AND SUPPORT EACH
OTHER. TO PROVIDE RESOURCES, SUPPORT, AND A SAFE HAVEN FOR
WOMEN.

Apostle Brazelton, Advisor

Pastor Duncan, Founder

Lady Haskins, Regional
For Texas

Email k.haskins0128@gmail.com | Contact: 346-599-1240

Bishop Anthony Williams and First Lady Modesta Williams are the Founder & Co-Founder of Living Vision Ministries located in Little Elm, Texas. Living Vision Ministries is devoted to spreading The Gospel of Jesus Christ through teaching the Biblical Principles, studying, and applying The Word of God in our day-to-day life, continuous prayer, and through Community and Global Outreach.

Bishop Williams is the Sr. Pastor of Living Vision Ministries; he holds a Doctoral Degree in Biblical Studies from Colorado Theological Seminary. He is a Preacher/Teacher who brings forth The Word of God with relevant scenarios and real-life experiences to help the next generation better understand His Word. Bishop Williams is a retired United States Navy Veteran. First Lady Modesta Williams spearheads the Women's Ministry, by teaching and showing teen girls and women how to be Women of God. She seeks to equip and encourage women to move beyond mediocrity and live the abundant life that is available for them through Jesus Christ.

Bishop Williams and First Lady Williams love spending time with their family; they are the proud parents of five children and four grandchildren. They like traveling, trying new restaurants, and shopping. Team Williams is a house divided; as it relates to Football, Bishop is a BIG Dallas Cowboys Fan, and the First Lady is a BIG Houston Texans Fan.

For more information regarding Living Vision Ministries please visit the website at www.lvministries.org or contact the Ministry at info@lvministries.org.

THE POWER OF GOD'S WORD
THE BOOK

LADY KATRINA HASKINS

Email k.haskins0128@gmail.com | Contact: 346-599-1240

AVAILABLE ON AMAZON

Master Plumber
Residential & Commercial
General Contractor
License of the city of Texas & Insured

NATURAL INGREDIENTS

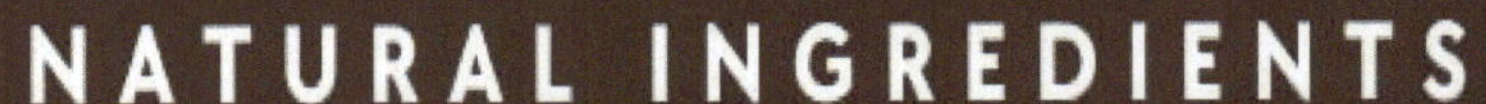

WHIPPED SOAPS BY NIKKI

936.346.1939

SEVERAL FRAGRANCES

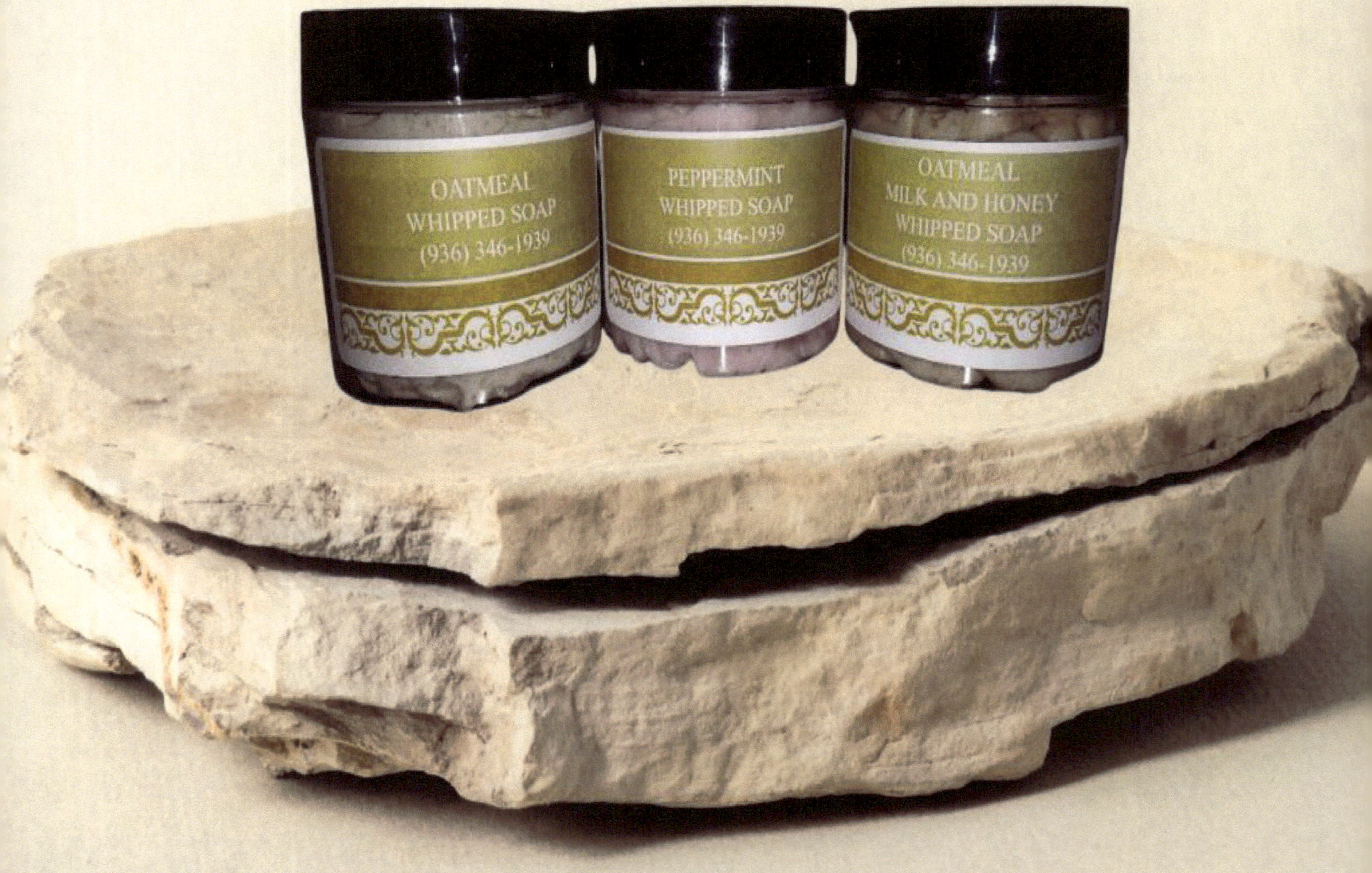

GET THE EDUCATION YOU'VE ALWAYS WANTED
YOUR DEGREE PLUS... INSPIRATION • IMPARTATION • ORDINATION!

Here's what our students are saying:

"I never pushed myself to study and go farther. Studying at LCU has awakened so much in my life." – S.S.

"LCU took my faith to a new level in God." – K.C.

"I've been to church all my life, and I thought I knew it all. But every course opens my eyes to more. The more I study, the more I realize there is so much more to learn!" – J.W.

"This is the best year of my life...and it's all because of LCU." – O.S.

"When God told me to come to LCU, I said, "God, this is me, Alex! Remember? The one who never liked school!" But the courses here are like nothing I've ever studied before. I look forward to every class and reading every book." – A.E.

ONLINE REVIEW: "LCU...maintains a high standard of educational quality, affordability, and convenience... The flexibility, convenience, and quality of these programs are the primary reason LCU has gained a reputation as one of the fastest growing theological institutions in the country." www.christiancolleges.com/school-reviews/life-christian-university/

IT'S ENJOYABLE!
•Earn an Associate, Bachelor, Master, or Doctoral degree while taking exciting, faith-filled courses)

IT'S AFFORDABLE!
• Undergraduate Tuition: $200 per month
• Graduate-level Tuition: $250 per month
• Textbooks are included with your tuition!

FOR MORE INFORMATION, CALL 903-374-1657
By Faith Ministries International of Baytown• 605 Massey Tompkins Suite C
• Baytown Texas
Mondays 7-10pm • New classes start every month: September to May!

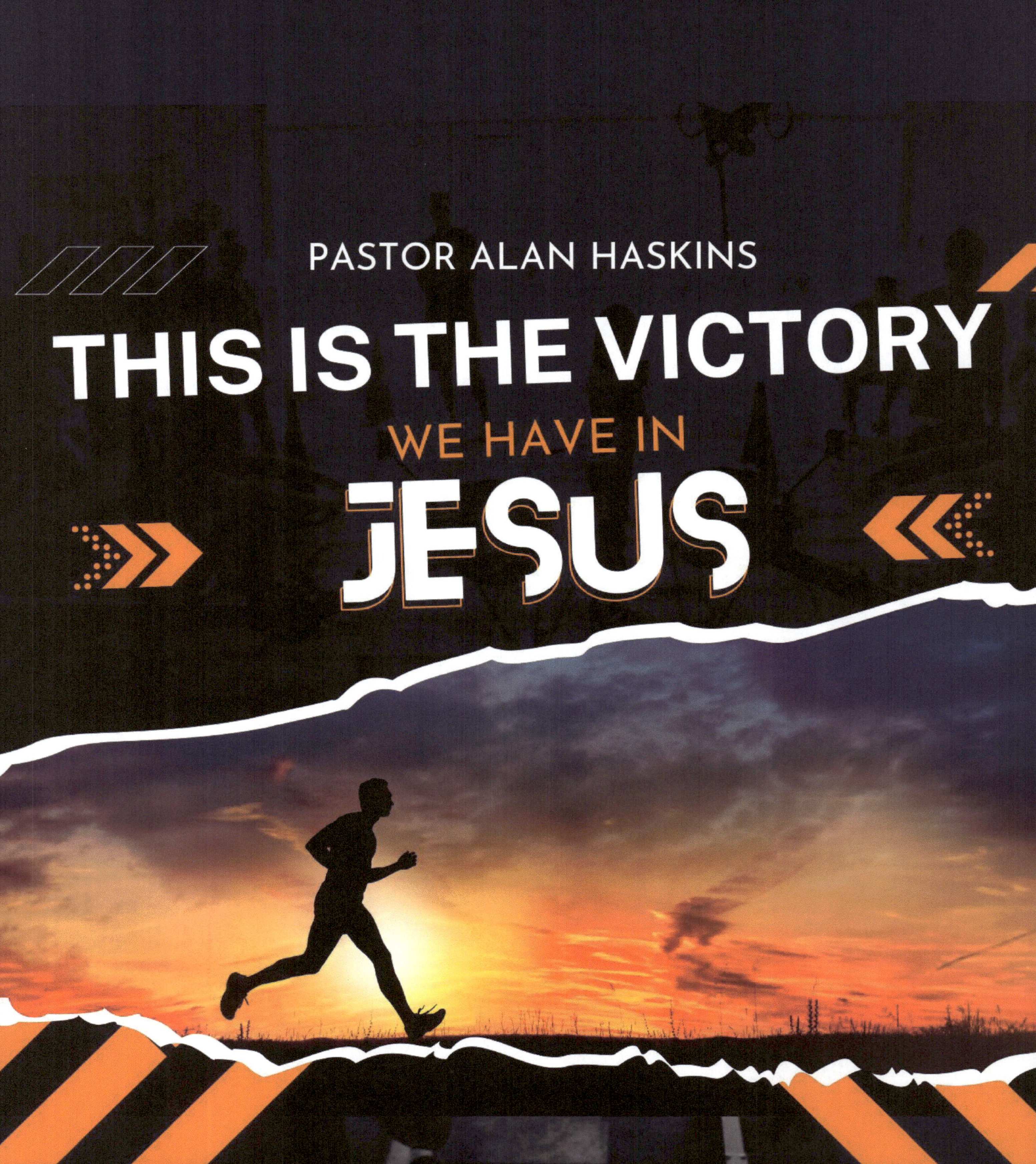

PASTOR ALAN HASKINS
THIS IS THE VICTORY
WE HAVE IN
JESUS

In life everybody wants the victory over something and some type of circumstance well 1st john :5,4, 6 states this is the victory that overcomes the world even our faith

one may not know what victory is. It is our coming or winning in competition or struggle over an opponent or difficult problem. The believer's opponent is the world and all its snares of life. snares are sickness family crises wages wars and more

How do we live? We live by faith principles that God has given us to trust him. This faith is trusting the word of God and what it says about our lives. This faith is the faith that helps and gives us strength , power and encouragement to live victorious in life.

even our faith, what faith? faith in Jesus Christ and the victory He has provided for the believers. four things faith does for us

1. faith makes all things possible
2. faith creates victory
3. faith gets to the root of all problem
4. faith is the helper for the believers to get the victory in life

The Hebrew writer says it this way: faith now means what you believe at that moment. you pray and ask God for it. the moment David said that he was going to the cut goliath head in 1st Samuel the angels went to work on Davids behalf

you must declare the ::word of God , the bible Saids death and life is in the power of your tongue proverbs. 18;21 you must speak you must open your mouth by faith and speak the powerful Word of God

prosper as you read
Pastor Alan Haskins

D.I.Y. CREDIT REPAIR

TAKE THE TIME TO
REPAIR YOUR CREDIT.
WE CAN
SHOW YOU HOW!

LADY KATRINA HASKINS

EXECUTIVE VICE PRES.

Email k.haskins0128@gmail.com

| Contact: 346-599-1240

Get Free In 2023!

Start Your Financial Breaktrough

MADELINE ALEXANDER

GET FREE IN 2023!

If you have ever felt that your financial battles are particularly intense, you are right! If you could pull back the veil and see clearly into the spiritual realm, you would quickly understand the battles that are raging over your finances. I will help you position yourself to win big financially, taking back everything the enemy has stolen and experiencing the peace of mind, abundance, and overflow the Lord Jesus has already secured for you at the cross.

In John 10:10 (AMPC) the Lord Jesus instructs us, *"The thief comes only in order to steal and kill and destroy. I came that they may have and enjoy life, and have it in abundance (to the full, till it overflows)."*

Your Heavenly Father wants you well and whole financially – able to amply provide for yourself and your family, prepare for the future, overcome unexpected challenges (like the COVID-19 pandemic), create financial freedom, leave an inheritance, build the Kingdom, and give generously to those in need. It is not God's intention for you to live paycheck-to-paycheck, under the strain of mounting debt, with stress and uncertainty concerning your financial future.

Proverbs 10:22 AMPC declares, *"The blessing of the Lord—it makes [truly] rich, and He adds no sorrow with it [neither does toiling increase it]."*

When you learn to build wealth God's way, you will eliminate the toiling, grinding, overwork, stress, and strain on your health and relationships.

Your financial battles are challenging because you are waging war on two fronts: in the spiritual realm and in the natural realm. As a believer and Kingdom citizen, the enemy is strategically targeting your finances as the front wave of a three-pronged coordinated attack, what I describe in detail as the Trifold Attack, in the book, *"Your 90 Day Financial Breakthrough: 90 Power Promises and the Weapons of Our Warfare to WIN In Your Finances Now."*

The enemy comes intentionally to steal your finances through poverty and lack, in order to stop the advancement of your purpose and Kingdom assignment. If he can hamstring you financially, little else will be accomplished. No matter how large your vision is, if you cannot finance it, it will be hindered to come to pass. Your vision requires provision, and the enemy desires to impede, interrupt, and intercept the flow of God's provision to your household and family.

Simultaneously, you are battling to overcome financial issues in the natural such as inflation, debt, and taxes, and systemic strongholds such as the race and gender wealth gap, all while striving to build wealth for your future, and a financial legacy for your family.

Without a clear and coordinated financial game plan that addresses both fronts, the spiritual and the natural, including the mentorship to guide you through challenging times, you could find yourself frustrated in a two-steps-forward, three-steps-backward cycle, frustrating your efforts to transform your financial future. But GOD! Be encouraged! There is HOPE!

GET FREE IN 2023!

I want to encourage you there is hope, help, and an open highway to financial security and blessing outlined in God's word! You have to make the decision to meet your financial challenges head-on, and do the work! Whether you are soaring, struggling, or stagnant right now, there is another level of financial blessing ahead for you, IF you make the commitment to be diligent to LEARN and EXECUTE! Here is a power promise for you in the Word of God.

"A lazy person's way is blocked with briers, but the path of the upright is an open highway." Proverbs 15:19 NLT

Make the decision to GET FREE in 2023! My ministry focus for this year is simple – GET FREE. I'm shouting from the rooftops to everyone it is time to GET FREE! Get debt-free, stress-free, and financially free in 2023. You can do it with the right system and help. You have to be intentional and follow the right system. As your coach, I will walk you through a proven system that will give you cashflow success and a blueprint to wealth that anyone can execute.

According to CNBC, 58% of Americans live paycheck to paycheck, including 36% of those earning at least $100,000 per year, and 30% of those earning $250,000 a year or more. Can you imagine earning a quarter of a million dollars a year and STILL living paycheck to paycheck? The culprits are taxes and debt.

Hosea 4:6 warns, *"My people are destroyed for lack of knowledge; because you have rejected knowledge, I reject you from being a priest to me."* Ouch! Don't stay in the dark financially. We must increase our spiritual knowledge and our financial toolkit to transform financially.

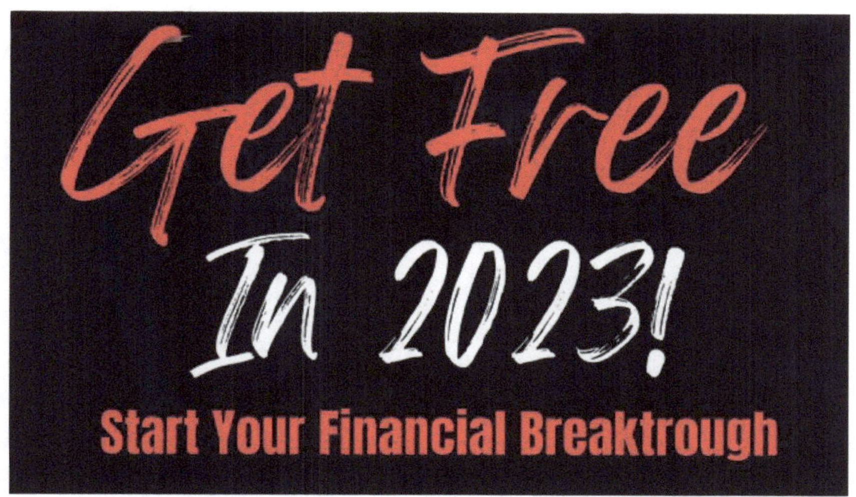

There are five core strategies you must learn to dramatically change your financial position:

1) **Cashflow** – learn how to immediately increase your cashflow and eliminate paycheck to paycheck living. 67% of African Americans live paycheck to paycheck. If you have a W-2 job, you can immediately correct this and keep more of your hard-earned money.

1) **Taxes** – taxes are your largest financial obligation annually. You must learn how to legally and ethically reduce your tax burden by leveraging the IRS tax code which rewards business ownership. Business ownership is a master key to wealth creation.

1) **Credit Repair** – bad credit will cost you a fortune! But don't despair, you can learn how to fix, manage, and maintain your own credit score with our DIY credit repair system, without hiring an expensive expert! Lower the cost of borrowing money for major purchases (house, car, etc.), and refinance high interest debts. Good credit is part of your debt elimination strategy.

1) **Debt Elimination** – the first wealth strategy in the word of God is to get out and stay out of debt. Proverbs 22:7 says, *"The rich rule over the poor, and the borrower is slave to the lender."* You want to get out of debt as fast as possible! You can learn how to accelerate debt payoff and live debt-fee!

1) **Investment Education** for Asset Accumulation – to get financially free, you must learn to build assets. This is the key to your retirement, or what I call freedom living. Freedom is not about age or income, it's all about asset accumulation. You can learn how to invest like the pros and build an asset portfolio to secure your freedom, even if you have never invested before.

Ready to get started? To learn what God's word says about your money, pick up a copy of *"Your 90 Day Financial Breakthrough."* It will transform your money mindset! It's available now on Amazon, or for a personally signed copy, go to www.ThePowerCoach.com.

To start on your Total Financial Solution, including strategies for cashflow, credit, taxes, debt, and investing, go to www.ProsperWithThePowerCoach.com, or contact Lady Katrina Haskins directly at https://KHaskins.myEcon.net. Get free in 2023!

• • • • • •

The Power Coach™ Madeline Alexander Barbee is America's premier rapid results success coach, helping Kingdom people prosper and build wealth God's way. Madeline is the author of "Your 90-Day Financial Breakthrough — 90 Power Promises and the Weapons of Our Warfare to WIN in Your Finances Now" and the top-selling inspirational series, "How to Break Through Barriers and Achieve Power Results; Create Your Power Mindset for Success in 30 Days or Less (Vol 1)" and "Power Mindset II: CHOOSE TO BE A CHAMPION (Vol 2)." An anointed minister of the gospel, and acclaimed motivational speaker, Madeline's pioneering, inspiring, and life-changing messages leave congregations strong, courageous, and mission minded! www.ThePowerCoach.com

Word Alive Ministries and Jerry Savelle Ministries Presents

SCHOOL OF FAITH

ONE YEAR COURSE. CLASSROOM SETTING. AND GRADUATION

STARTING 5th March 2023
Time: 6pm-8pm

Developing a Passion for God
Principles of Prayer
Principles of Living by Faith
The Character of God
Biblical Prosperity
Fruit of the Spirit
There's Power in the Blood

REGISTRATION FEE:

$99 monthly for 5 months

Class Instructors:
Dr. Alan Haskins
and Pastor Katrina Haskins

209 East Texas Ave.
Baytown, Texas 77521

Submission Link
www.wordaliveministries.biz

More Information: 832.457.5981 or 346.599.1240

LOOKING FOR AN AGENT?

"We are the key to your next move."

GREATER MT CARMEL CHURCH
Join us every Sunday @11am
@ 7414 Wheatley St. Houston
TX 77088
BISHOP GEORGE SANDERS
PROPHETESS LATRESA SANDERS

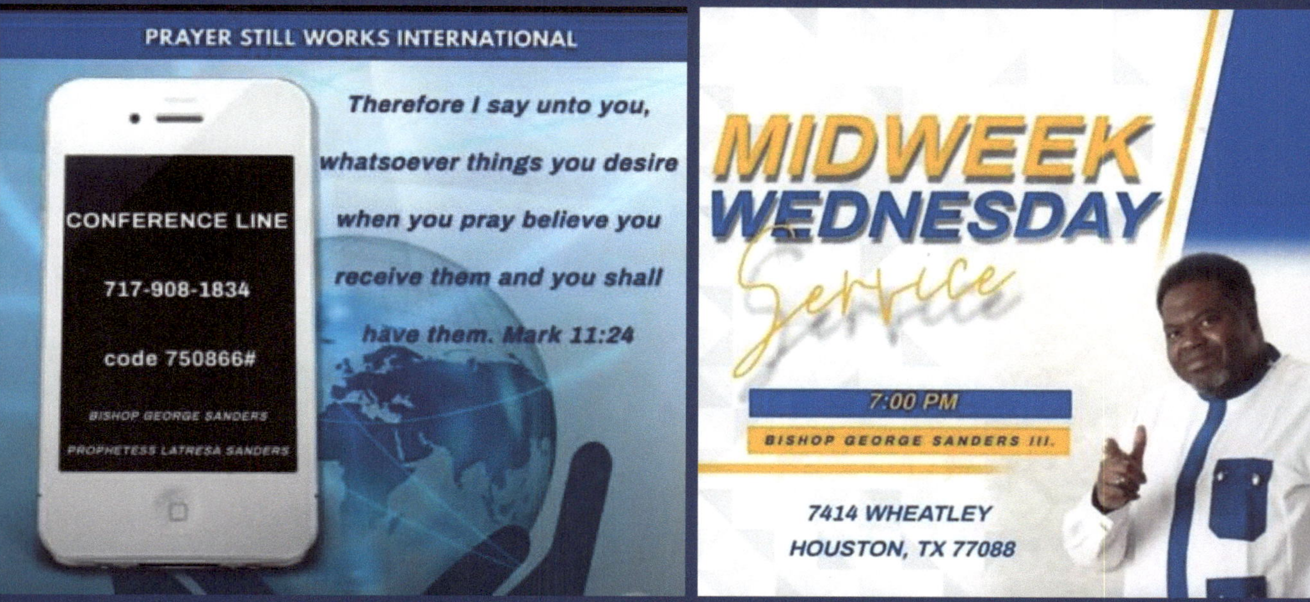
PRAYER STILL WORKS INTERNATIONAL
Therefore I say unto you, whatsoever things you desire when you pray believe you receive them and you shall have them. Mark 11:24
CONFERENCE LINE
717-908-1834
code 750866#
BISHOP GEORGE SANDERS
PROPHETESS LATRESA SANDERS
MIDWEEK WEDNESDAY Service
7:00 PM
BISHOP GEORGE SANDERS III.
7414 WHEATLEY
HOUSTON, TX 77088

THE ALLIANCE MARKETING GROUP

Insurance

- ✓ WHOLE LIFE
- ✓ TERM LIFE
- ✓ CHILDREN
- ✓ ANNUITIES
- ✓ IUL

Call Now

KATRINA HASKINS, INSURANCE BROKER
346.599.1240
CAREER OPPORTUNITIES

DEAR GOD,

I NEED YOU,
I AM HUMBLY CALLING OUT TO YOU,
I'M TIRED OF DOING THINGS MY WAY.
HELP ME TO START DOING THINGS YOUR WAY,
I INVITE YOU INTO MY LIFE TO BE
MY LORD AND SAVIOR,
FILL THE EMPTINESS IN ME WITH YOUR
HOLY SPIRIT AND MAKE ME WHOLE.
LORD, HELP ME TO TRUST YOU,
HELP ME TO LOVE YOU,
HELP ME TO LIFE FOR YOU
HELP ME TO UNDERSTAND YOUR GRACE,
YOUR MERCY, AND YOUR PEACE.
THANK YOU LORD,

SUNDAY
Service
@11AM

209 EAST TEXAS AVE.
BAYTOWN, TEXAS 77520
832.457.5981
346.599.1240

PASTOR ALAN &
LADY KATRINA
HASKINS

"A PLACE WHERE CLOTHES
DOESN'T MATTER, THE
SOULS MATTER."

WWW.WORDALIVEMINISTRIES.BIZ

DOT'S PLACE

4 2 4 3 1